I Can't Help Being an INFP Writer

Arcadia Page

Published by Arcadia Page, 2020.

I CAN'T HELP BEING AN INFP WRITER

First edition. October 8, 2020.

ISBN: 978-1393722090

Written by Arcadia Page.

Also by Arcadia Page

Watch for more at www.arcadiapage.com.

Table of Contents

Getting Started

At the age of four, I was introduced to writing stories. My mom had already taught me to read and write, and my dad had fun creating little short stories with me.

At that age, I already loved reading, so learning how to create stories of my own had an everlasting impact on my life.

I saw writing as a way to create worlds that were different from the one I lived in. I could save the movies in my mind on paper and replay them as many times as I wanted.

Writing also made it possible for me to save important concepts so I could refer to them later. One of my earliest works of nonfiction? *How to Cook Oatmeal.* It was a little illustrated booklet created from notebook paper stapled together.

As I grew up, writing became a way to document observations, what I'm learning, and my life. Writing has helped me to observe, think, dream, and build my identity in private.

What has writing done for you?

This book grew out of a much shorter blog post entitled Thoughts on How I Work as an INFP Writer[1], and I'm excited to share this with you.

If you're expecting a book that tells you exactly how to write, well, that's not what's happening here. Instead, the goal of this book is to start you on the journey of uncovering your process.

Writing is an art. There are as many ways to paint a brushstroke on canvas as there are artists in the world. The same goes for methods of putting words onto a page.

---

1. https://arcadiapage.com/2019/10/thoughts-on-how-i-work-as-infp-writer.html

The suggestions here center on capturing ideas, staying motivated, and overcoming problems. In this book, I often refer to personality type functions.

As a short reference, INFP functions work in the following order:

1. Introverted Feeling

2. Extroverted Intuition

3. Introverted Sensing

4. Extroverted Thinking

Sometimes the function stack of the INFP shows up in books and web articles as FiNeSiTe.

Introverted Feeling (Fi) and Extroverted Intuition (Ne) are our strongest functions. Introverted Sensing and Extroverted Thinking (Si and Te) are our weaker functions. To learn more about how MBTI functions work, a great place to start is Personality Junkie[2] by Dr. A.J. Drenth. You don't have to understand functions to benefit from this book, but learning a little more about them can help.

Here, I explore the workings of the INFP writer function by function. I hope from my exploration, you'll find deeper insight into what you can do.

I arranged this book into a long list that's broken up into chapters. This will make it easier to note the ideas that speak to you and integrate them into your process.

Also, you don't have to read this book in order. You can skip to any section that fits what you need at the moment.

---

2. https://personalityjunkie.com/myers-briggs-functions-inferior-function/

I've read tons of non-fiction, and I find that I'm gravitating more towards books that encourage me to take action. I would love to see you make progress on your projects instead of getting bogged down in another "How-to-Write" book.

In fact, I encourage you to pull out a work in progress, an old piece of writing, or start something new as you go through this book. The best way to see where you are and need to grow is to actively write.

I hope INFP writer, that this book will help you to take action and overcome setbacks.

Mindset: Your Feelings Matter

In the INFP function stack, Introverted Feeling is at the top.

Introverted Feeling is the function INFPs are the most comfortable with. In fact, Introverted Feeling is probably one of the main reasons why many INFPs love writing. Writing allows us to express ourselves and sort through our inner world.

Part of Introverted Feeling involves figuring out what is and isn't meaningful. For me, writing is meaningful, so I do it as often as I can. But chores don't hold much meaning for me, so I tend to avoid them. What's meaningful varies from INFP to INFP, so two INFPs can have different values.

Another part of Introverted Feeling is measuring the distance of relationships. It helps us to feel the emotional space that's between us and others. It also helps us to notice how close or far people are from each other. I'm often driven to close the gaps I sense in my personal relationships, doing whatever I can to feel closer when the distance bothers me.

But at some point, close is too close, and I need to create some space. It's as if there's a circle drawn around me. Sometimes people are too far away from the line, and I wish they were closer. Other times, they are too near the line, and I need them to back away.

Introverted Feeling cares about internal harmony and how things feel within. It takes a focused view of relationships, paying more attention to one-on-one interactions.

Introverted Feeling is a great tool for writing because it's aware of the intricacies of character interactions. This is an advantage for INFP fiction writers.

Introverted Feeling also is important for gaining and maintaining motivation. If you are losing motivation for your work or are dealing with flat characters, bring Introverted Feeling into the mix and see what happens.

Below is a list of suggestions on how to bring Introverted Feeling into your process and improve your mindset.

1 - Keep a journal. Make it a place where you're free to express yourself. Write and draw whatever you want. Also, take the time to re-read your journals. While journal writing can feel messy, the insights you discover when re-reading may amaze you. Doing stream-of-conscious journaling weekly for at least 15 minutes has helped me to hear my writer's voice and feel mentally organized.

2 - Set aside a day with no plans. People who use Introverted Feeling must have moments of unstructured time. This month, make space for a day that has zero plans. Instead, use it for exploring, dreaming, reflecting, and creating.

3 - Embody your main character. If you're writing fiction, take time to imagine that you're living the life of your main character.

What do you look like? Where do you live? How do you communicate? Do you have a job? What is your family like? How does it feel to be in their body? What is it like going through certain story moments? What is it like interacting with other characters through their point of view?

As you take a walk in their shoes, also be aware of the emotions they feel towards their life. Try doing the same with other characters as well.

4 - Reflect on all the times you've written in private and created work only for yourself. Was it in a journal? In a bare-bones Word document with a special font? Were you writing outside, in a comfy chair or in bed? Were you writing poetry between your class notes in school? Think about your most private writing moments.

5 - Recreate your experience of writing in private. It's important to find the space that helps you to bring out your authentic writing, not the voice you think you "should" use. Were you a between-biology-notes writer? Then take your writing to a coffee shop or a library and scribble in a composition notebook. Do your best to recreate your experience of writing privately.

6 - Imagine how a good writing session feels. Where are you? What do you see? What do you hear? How are you sitting? If you're struggling to create the picture in your mind, write your answers to these questions.

7 - Reflect on why you love to write. What role has writing played in your life?

8 - Reconnect with why your project is meaningful. When we start dealing with the nuts and bolts of a project, we can forget all about why this idea captured our interest in the first place. So ask yourself, "What does this project mean to me? What do I want to get out of it? What is it about this project that makes me excited? What do I want readers to get out of it?

9 - Stay aware of the connection between you and your writing project. While planning a project, ask yourself, "How does this project relate to me? How is this related to topics, ideas, objects, people, places, or anything else that fascinates me? What do I want to express or share?"

Does your writing project move your heart? Make sure that what you write is meaningful to you.

If you let Introverted Feeling guide you, you'll abandon projects less often. Each project you take on will align with your identity, giving you an extra boost of motivation.

10 - Follow what has personal value. Sometimes we get so caught up in what's interesting, that we forget to check if it's valuable to us. When you're losing your way because of chasing new ideas, take a moment to ask yourself, "Where am I trying to go? Will this idea take me there? "

11 - Use your feelings to keep moving on a writing project. If you feel you need to take your writing in a certain direction, go with it and see where it takes you. Introverted Feeling is an effective creative compass.

12 - Sit with your feelings. If you're working on a piece of writing and something doesn't feel right, ask yourself, "What do I dislike about this? What is valuable to me when it comes to this piece? What is not?" You may have to take some quiet time to sort it all out. Then keep what is valuable and remove the rest.

Recently, I was working on a story, and it started feeling icky to me. By doing the above, I realized that I didn't care for the setting or the characters. So I changed all that I didn't like.

13 - Make your feelings number one in your process. In a world of writing as a business, it seems having a factory mindset is on the rise. Plug characters, setting, and internal motivations into a formula, and out comes a book. These formulas can be helpful when troubleshooting story problems. But, those internal tugs you feel of what's not working in your story are way more important than formulas.

No two pieces of writing are identical. A process that may have been great for creating one piece may fail with another. So if something doesn't feel right, look into that, even if it goes against formal structures and writing blueprints.

14 - If a piece of writing advice is a bad fit, let it go. Don't try to stick to it because that's what works for [insert name of a crazy successful writer]. As INFPs, our personal values dictate our process, not other people.

15 - Don't beat yourself up over unfinished work. It's more helpful to learn from it and see if you could do better next time. If you stop on a project, ask yourself, "What did I learn from it? What didn't work? What worked? What did this project teach me about what kind of writing that fits me? What could I do differently next time?"

16 - Realize that your unpublished writing can have an unexpected impact. I wrote my first novel when I was 15. After writing it, I shared it with a few friends, but since then I've kept it in a binder unpublished. Recently a friend told me that reading the novel I wrote way back then inspired her to get into writing. And when I shared it with my husband while we were dating, he said that after reading it, he knew I was the right girl for him.

17 - Remember that anything you write can change lives. Writing is powerful, and its power goes beyond the act of publishing. What we write can impact others, even if it NEVER sees the book store or public internet. So if you write something that you're not ready to publish, don't feel ashamed of that. Instead, share it with a few close friends. Or read it aloud in a locked room to share it with yourself. It may impact you and others in ways you don't expect.

Ideas & Running After Shiny Things

In the function stack of INFPs, Extroverted Intuition is second in command. It is your idea machine. Extroverted Intuition (Ne) combines concepts and inspiration. It's about being curious, finding new ideas, and bringing them together in unique ways.

Introverted Feeling and Extroverted Intuition are often partnered together. When Introverted Feeling sees an idea, it's like, "Oh, that concept is meaningful to me. I want to dig deeper into it. "

Then Extroverted Intuition goes, "Okay, here's all the ideas and possibilities related to that one idea."

It's similar to typing a single term into a search engine and getting pages of results, some more related to the original idea than others. And just how it's easy to fall into the dark abyss of browsing the internet for hours, it's not unusual to get lost in the tangle of ideas provided by Extroverted Intuition. This can make plotting stories or creating outlines challenging.

Extroverted Intuition is also distracting. For me, testing writing apps, playing with name generators, and collecting Pinterest pins can be a total rush. Yet, those activities aren't helping me to make tangible progress on my projects. One of the main markers of Extroverted Intuition is the trail of unfinished work it leaves behind.

This function is fast, intense, divergent, non-linear, and organizes things into an interconnected web instead of in categories.

Despite all that, Extroverted Intuition is your messy, crazy, and unpredictable best friend. It's the function that makes ideas grow. It's what turns that one sentence idea into 500 pages and counting. The goal isn't to subdue Extroverted Intuition. It works better when it's given room to run with a little direction.

That direction is often given by Introverted Feeling. Remember, Introverted Feeling carries what is valuable and essential to you. It can help you to know where to go despite the impulses of Extroverted Intuition (See points 10 and 24).

Here is some more advice for doing the dance with Extroverted Intuition as a writer.

18 - Bring together your ideas and fascinations. Build a collection of notes or notebooks that spark your imagination. Allowing some messiness will help you to combine your ideas in unique ways.

Yet, do the best you can to collect your ideas in a common place. Then when you're ready to start your draft, bring them all together.

Read through your notes and highlight the most important and exciting ideas related to your project. Then type those ideas into a document, and save them in the same folder as your rough draft.

19 – Go beyond writing about what you know. Write about what makes you curious. Engage with what you want to learn more about. Explore new things.

20 - Pay attention to what ideas from movies, video games, fiction, and so on, appeal to you. Also, watch out for small details in story settings or minor characters.

Write down anything interesting you see. It may be a useful element in a future project.

21 - Get inspiration from what you appreciate. Pay attention to real-life people, places, things, and concepts you find interesting. If you find it difficult to connect with daily life, note the everyday things you appreciate.

Do you appreciate your socks? Your daily coffee cup? After listing a few things, create an essay, short story, poem, or song about one of them. You can branch out and do the same thing with people and places you encounter.

22 - Mix and match what inspires you. If you like the personality of one character and the profession of another, what would happen if you combined them? Do the same with settings, plot lines, themes and so on.

23 - Collect online information you find interesting with a web clipper browser extension. I've found this to be a great way to collect resources for future reference while writing.

24 - If you're overwhelmed with ideas, bring in Introverted Feeling. As you work on your project, ask yourself, "What does writing do for me? What makes this project meaningful?" Make sure your ideas align with your values and goals.

25 - Make the most of your new writing project ideas. When you get an idea for a new project, write more than a few words about it. Avoid saving ideas with so little detail that when you return to them, it's hard to figure out what you had in mind. The goal is to have enough written so that the concept isn't lost when you return to it.

Try free-writing a page or two. Free-write about the story or the story itself.

26 - Add flexibility to your writing practice. More than likely, you'll end up fitting writing around your day job, classes at school, or the crazy randomness of life. Ask yourself, "What small breaks or quiet moments do I have throughout the day? How can I use those moments for writing instead of checking social media or other non-essential things?"

If you want to make writing on the go more comfortable, create a list of what would be in your ideal writing environment. Then brainstorm how you could take parts of that experience with you wherever you go. Do you dream of working in quiet isolation? Buy a pair of noise isolating earphones. Get creative with ways to make your writing experience portable.

27 - Create a mindmap of characters, so you can see the connections between them. If you're writing fiction, take a moment to see how your characters connect to each other. Do some characters wish to be closer to others but are having a hard time closing the gap? If some characters don't have a connection, what do you think would happen if they did? If they met each other, even once, what would happen? Do any of your characters' relationships mimic the ones you've observed in your life?

28 - Try writing stories like TV shows, ending each chapter with a "what will happen next?" I've found that working with episodes creates less pressure because it gives me more room to plan the twist. It also keeps me motivated and gives me freedom to end stories whenever I'm ready. For more about how I write this way, check out my blog post Using Your Writer's Intuition to Plan Fiction[1].

29 - Use your unfinished projects as jumping-off points for better work. Unfinished work receives so much negativity. Like everyone, I have projects I've abandoned. But to me, none of my half-done projects were pointless.

Brainstorm, using your unfinished work as inspiration. Pull out an abandoned piece of writing and make a list of all the ideas and concepts from the project you appreciate, including specific words, names, and situations. If it's fiction, also include which characters and settings you like. Then on a fresh page, using your list as inspiration, write about what new directions you could explore.

---

1. https://arcadiapage.com/2018/10/using-your-writers-intuition-to-plan.html

30 - Get creative with unfinished work. Print out your unfinished work. Try cutting it up paragraph-by-paragraph and rearranging it into something new. Or cut out words from your unfinished work and transform them into found poetry or a song. If you're a visual artist, see what happens if you cut up your writing and use it in a painting or some other medium.

31 - Although unfinished work happens, try to finish your projects. It may mean writing an ending you hate, and that's okay. You can always change it. Plus, by writing what you fear (which is in this case, something terrible), you free your mind to consider better options. If you let the fear of messing up keep you from moving forward, you will miss the chance to find solutions. You can't fix what you don't write.

32 - If you're sick of a story, slap any old ending on it. As the writer, you are free to end the story however you want.

If you're scared to do this, list all the horrible movies or books that you've encountered. Think about how they generated income for someone. Bad writing is not a life or death matter. Some things you make will be great and some won't. But, be more discerning than the people on your list about what to publish and what could use some extra time.

33 - Build appreciation for short projects. Many writers view publishing that novel or book as the pinnacle of the craft. Unfortunately, this viewpoint can cause us to forget that shorter works have merit. Especially as someone who uses Extroverted Intuition, it can be hard to commit to creating a long piece of work.

If you're struggling with focus, try one of these short projects:

34 - Write a poem.

35 - Make a zine.

36 - Write a short story.

37 - Write a novella.

38 - Write an article or essay.

39 - Write a song.

40 - Write flash fiction.

41 - Write a script for a one-chapter comic or short play.

42 - Build collections of your short projects. If you make enough small projects, you can create a themed collection of them. A collection doesn't have to be all poetry or flash fiction. You can bring together a mix of whatever you want. And that could end up being the book you've always wanted to write.

43 - Use short projects to solve larger story problems. If I'm struggling with a big piece of writing, creating a related short work can help me to solve the problems. Short projects give me insight, helping me find unexpected sources of direction.

44 - If you feel the urge to grow your short projects, don't resist it. Not all short stories should become novels, and not all poetry will fit into a collection. But if you create something short, and your mind keeps spinning out ideas of how to make it bigger, go for it. That means you've hit the tip of the iceberg, and it's worth exploring.

Getting Writing Done

As INFPs, Introverted Sensing and Extroverted Thinking are our less-developed functions. Introverted Sensing is third and Extroverted Thinking is fourth.

Fi Ne **Si Te**

Yet, both of them play a key role in helping us to take action and finish our writing projects. Let's take a quick tour of these functions.

Introverted Sensing

Introverted Sensing involves routine, traditions, appreciating past methods, and nostalgia. It also involves the mind-body connection, bringing awareness to internal physical sensations. People with Introverted Sensing tend to enjoy solitary physical activities and appreciate routine.

Since it's third in the function stack of INFPs, it's not as powerful as Introverted Feeling or Extroverted Intuition. So, it's typical for INFPs to struggle with sticking to routines.

We have this inner tension between the old and the new. Extroverted Intuition looks for the latest and greatest possibilities. But Introverted Sensing wants to stick with what works and preserve the past. Often, we end up blending both together.

Although it's not one of our strong points, Introverted Sensing can be a great ally to the writing process of INFPs. It can help us to slow the flow of new ideas so that we can focus on the here and now of writing.

In fact, the third function in the stack is often called the "relief" function. That means when you're tired and stressed, you can turn to this function to feel balanced again. Many INFPs find balance by doing mind-body exercise, savoring favorite foods, and enjoying favorite childhood books, movies, and cherishing fond memories. For more about using Introverted Sensing for stability, I recommend reading **Tranquility by Type** by Susan Storm.

We don't want to lean on Introverted Sensing too much because as a weaker function, it can wear out easily, causing us problems. If you feel stuck in a rut, more than likely you've exhausted Introverted Sensing. But we do want to make use of it the INFP way.

Using Introverted Sensing will bring balance to your writing process. It helps with creating focus and releasing internal worries and pressure.

Extroverted Thinking

Extroverted Thinking is our inferior function. It involves using existing external systems to get things done. People who primarily use Extroverted Thinking rely on having a plan and making things happen. They want to see results and solutions, removing any inefficiencies they notice. They are interested in managing time, people, money, and their external environment in general. Extroverted Thinking is the boss.

Since it's at the bottom of the function stack for INFPs, that means we have the least access to it. It's not uncommon for INFPs to struggle with external order, making plans to reach their goals, and telling others what to do.

It also means that it's the function we default to when lashing out in anger to defend ourselves or are having a bad day. I know that when I'm stressed, I become obsessed about having everything "under control," and I get unusually irritated when people don't do what I tell them to.

The inferior function, despite being the weakest, can also be alluring. Often people imagine, "If I could conquer that weak spot, then I'll be whole." Sometimes we're completely unaware of our attraction to

Extroverted Thinking, but it's that attraction that moves some INFPs to take up jobs that involve working daily with external systems and logic, such as in the sciences or business management. I have a degree in computer engineering and a strong entrepreneurial streak. On paper, I can appear to be an Extroverted Thinking type, but I'm not.

We don't want to lean too much on our inferior function. If we do, we risk falling into the "grip" of it, or under its control. As INFPs, we don't want to live the life of an angry, under-developed ESTJ, which is what happens when we fall into the grip. Plus, when we rely too much on Extroverted Thinking, we can become rigid in our thoughts and ideas. We want to stay our free-flowing selves. We're not as skilled at using Extroverted Thinking as a healthy ESTJ.

However, bringing a touch of Extroverted Thinking into our process can be the perfect kick in the butt to keep on track with our projects. Also critiquing and seeing how things are measuring up to set standards is a strong part of Extroverted Thinking. Extroverted Thinking is your internal writing coach and editor.

Use Your Tools

As an INFP, it may be difficult to put a writing system or method in place, since we struggle with sticking to routines and systems in general. But what we can do is build a personal set of tools that we can take in hand at different parts of the process like an artist who knows which brush to use.

This mindset fits well with the way INFPs handle information. Since INFPs rely on Extroverted Intuition, we value flexibility. Being able to grab the right tool when needed is more flexible than trying to work according to a system.

This chapter brings it all together. It not only shows how you can use your primary and secondary functions of Introverted Feeling and

Extroverted Intuition to get writing done, but it also brings the qualities of Introverted Sensing and Extroverted Thinking into play.

As you read, pay attention to which ideas seem the most promising when it comes to keeping forward momentum on your writing projects.

You may need different tools for different projects. You may need many tools for the same problem. A specific tool may not work all the time depending on the circumstances. But regardless, don't neglect to build your personal set of tools.

Here are more tips for getting writing done.

45 - Just get started. It can be way too easy to fall into procrastination. Procrastination keeps telling us that we need one more piece of information before starting our project. The outline needs to be adjusted a tiny bit more before we can try...

But deep within, we know the difference between doing needed research and putting things off. If you have everything together for your project but are facing the stage-fright of the blank page, start by setting a 5-minute timer. Then for those 5 minutes, type as much of your project as you can.

Often when it comes to things that I struggle to start, I find that 5 minutes of giving it a try is enough for me to realize that I am ready for this.

You are more ready than you think you are.

46 - Don't let the fear of plotting or structure hold you back from getting started. It's easy to make the structure of a writing project more complex than it needs to be. From doing so much writing, I've found that the more I simplify the structure, the less overwhelmed I feel, and the easier it is to get it done (This book is a great example. It's nothing more than a detailed list).

Every time I start a blog post, I start with the question, "What are the three main points I want to cover?" I start with a three-item list and that grows into a blog post.

I recently plotted a small novel that I want to write the same way. I asked myself, "What are the main events I want to cover in my story?" I limited my list to 7 – 10 main events. I made sure this list was a snapshot of the entire story, from beginning to end.

Under some of the events, I made brief notes about character introductions and other important details.

My favorite things about this method is that it made it easy to:

- Note the scenes/moments that were stuck on replay in my mind.
- Arrange those moments into a chronological order that made sense.
- Get a feel of the plot structure and move major events around.
- Spot and correct a plot fallacy.
- See how to start the main story without getting bogged down in backstory.
- Reduce fluff
- Create a framework that allows me to embrace spontaneity, but yet stay on track with where I want the story to go.

I definitely expect my outline to grow from 10 plot points, but it's a good starting point.

If you desire more advice on plotting simplicity, I recommend checking out **Writing Without Rules** by Jeffery Somers, which I describe in more detail in the Resources & Conclusion chapter.

47 - Create urgency. When I was working on my webcomic, I had to complete two pages per week to meet my posting schedule. Over time I've found that aiming to have something done by the end of the week creates enough pressure for me to work on it daily. I think it comes from having most of my assignments in school due on Friday.

The only other due date I respond to is "by the end of the month." Anything further out than that is not compelling.

Another way I create urgency is by using, "If I do this, then I can do that." It's similar to when parents say, "If you do your homework, then you can have some ice cream."

I enjoy telling myself, "If you write a chapter of your book, then you can spend the rest of your evening reading." Sounds good to me!

Think back to times when you met a due date without feeling overly pressured. What helped you to make consistent progress?

48 - Page count and word count are overrated. Stories suffer when the writer forces them into being a certain length. Stories forced into being novels are often filled with time-wasting filler. Stories forced to be shorter have convenient plot fallacies.

In nonfiction, books that are padded to be longer often suffer from repetitive information.

49 - Accept whatever your writing becomes. You may write one sentence and be done with it. Or you may write hundreds of pages. Don't suffer through a story. End it when you feel done with it. It's okay if it turns into a short story instead of a novel. Or a piece of flash fiction instead of a short story.

50 - Create a list of typical distractions you face while writing. Family, nagging chores, neighbors mowing the lawn, Instagram, your buzzing phone...write them all down. After noting possible distractions, take a few moments to brainstorm things you can do to keep them from encroaching on your writing time.

51 - Create a list of other problems you could face while writing. Is it a lack of motivation? Feelings of fear and uncertainty? Plot issues? Flat characters? Write down the problems that pose roadblocks to your writing. Then do research and make notes on what you can do to work around them. Write those notes in your inspiration notebook.

52 - Be aware of how you tend to write. Do you naturally write in pieces that need to be organized later? Do you lean towards splitting up your project into many documents? Or do you spill everything into one big document?

53 - Use software that matches your process. I am a writer who lets it all out in one document. I've been doing so since childhood. I've tried using Scrivener, but I found it too overpowered for my process. So my writing apps of choice are programs like Microsoft Word and WPS Writer. I also enjoy using minimalist apps that allow me to jump around in the same document, such as Focus Writer[1] and Left[2].

Currently, Left is my favorite writing app. I wrote this entire book using Left. The minimal interface helps me to focus, and it's designed to keep my fingers on the keyboard, not the mouse. I love the different themes. Plus managing the different sections of my document and the other projects I'm working on has been amazingly simple.

If you're a writer who writes in pieces, you may find apps that can handle many documents at once to be a good fit. Scrivener is the first that comes to mind. Left and Typora[3] are minimalist apps that also handle multiple

---

1. https://gottcode.org/focuswriter/

2. https://100r.co/site/left.html

3. https://typora.io/

documents. Obsidian[4] is also worth checking out. Regardless of what you choose, pick writing apps that fit your natural process.

54 - Bring a hands-on element to your writing. At some point, use pen and paper. It can be for capturing ideas, planning details, outlining, or editing. It doesn't matter when you choose to use paper, but at some point, write by hand. Introverted Sensing is about connecting your mind with your body, and when you hand-write, you are bringing balance and calm into your writing process.

55 - Have comfortable lighting in your writing space. Not having appropriate lighting can hurt your concentration and lead to eye strain.

56 - Use a blue light filter on your screens. Don't let your writing practice disturb your sleep. Turn on night mode or install a blue light filter app. I've found the Iris Mini app[5] to be a simple solution for this.

57 - Use comfortable pens and a comfortable keyboard. And the most comfortable chair you can find. Writing should be enjoyable, not painful.

58 - Create a calming environment for concentration. What counts as a calm environment varies from person to person. Some people need a little noise or music. Others need absolute silence. Pay attention to what you see, smell, and hear in your writing environment. Are any of those things distracting? Is there anything you can add to make things more pleasant? Remove what's distracting and bring in what's enjoyable.

Extra tip: Where I live, I have a neighbor across the street who plays loud music. I can easily hear it in my house. In the past, I tuned it out with a good set of earplugs. But lately, I've discovered the web app Calmyleon[6]. Their white noise setting works great at making unwanted noises disappear.

---

4. https://obsidian.md/

5. https://iristech.co/iris-mini/

6. https://calmyleon.com/

59 - Prepare before you write. If you know that during your writing session you will want a snack or some coffee, get those things together before you start. I used to stop in the middle of my writing session to make a snack and brew coffee, but I've realized that stopping hurts my momentum. It's better that I keep going and have those extra comforts nearby. Use the restroom before you start as well.

View your writing time as going on a road trip. Prepare all you need before you get on the road to make the trip smooth and enjoyable. Get what makes you comfortable, set out your writing tools, and bring out whatever kinds of maps you plan to use, such as outlines and research materials. The popular idea of having a "writing ritual" is nothing more than creating a method of preparation that fits you.

60 - Keep your routine simple. Decide if you're going to write every day, five days a week, or only on the weekends. If you find writing regularly a challenge, try:

- Writing daily for 15 to 20 minutes before breakfast. Or before going to bed.
- Write as if you're taking medication. This schedule is from *The Writer's Space* by Eric Maisel. Instead of having one writing session of 10 to 20 minutes have four throughout the day: 8 AM, 12 PM, 4 PM, 8 PM. This is great for when it's hard to find time to do a solid hour of writing.
- Doing a mini-Pomodoro. Do 10 minutes of writing. Take a 5-minute break. Then do 10 more minutes of writing. Then reward yourself at the end of the session. This is a nice way to get work done when you're not feeling well.

I have used all these methods, and they have helped me to make progress on my projects even when facing challenges such as working in retail or suffering from depression.

61 - Figure out how to write wherever you are as often as you can. Artists often carry a sketchbook so that they can create art no matter where they are. Take the same approach with your writing.

62 - Test out writing everywhere. Don't wait for the perfect environment. Although it's important to set up an environment at home to serve as your base, the reality is that often you have to create the perfect environment where ever you are, whenever you have a free moment. You can make writing on the go more comfortable by having materials that are easy to carry and are in reach. Take aromatherapy and calming music with you. Use a book light if you're often in the dark.

63 - Don't let the lack of pen and paper stop you. Remember that you can always work on your writing project in your mind whenever you want. Never discount the power of using contemplation to work through your story. Taking time to think deeply about your writing project always pays off, even if you can't note down your insights at the moment.

64 - Experiment with saving your writing projects in plain text or markdown files. Writing with plain text isn't for everyone, but what I love about plain text files is that they are simple to work with, there are zero formatting issues when switching between writing applications, and the format is timeless. A plain text file created in the '90s can still be read today–as long as those files were moved from a floppy disk to a USB drive at some point.

65 - Learn markdown. Markdown is a special way of formatting a plain text document. Its purpose is to make it possible for writers to work in a variety of programs without having to fight with formatting issues. Keyboard symbols are used to show different kinds of formatting so that making a section bold or italicized does not break the flow of typing. In fact, markdown makes it possible for writers to type and add formatting without having to remove their fingers from the keyboard. Visit

TheMarkdownGuide.org[7] for more information on formatting with markdown.

66 - Try apps that support markdown. All the apps I've mentioned before, Obsidian, Typora, and Left, support markdown. Good online apps to try are Calmly Writer[8], Draft[9], and Ginko[10]. Trello isn't made for extensive writing, but it also supports markdown in the description boxes of each card.

67 - If you're having a difficult time focusing on writing, get in touch with your mind and body. If you're struggling to focus, that means you need a break. You could take a break by reading emails or social media, but below are some more mindful ways of taking a break that will engage Introverted Sensing. Using your Introverted Sensing to refill will not only give you a better sense of balance, but it will allow your mind to work with ideas in a relaxed way.

68 - Repetitive drawing. Fill a blank page with lines, dots, or shapes. Use a pen or paint.

69 - Exercise. Do your favorite workout. If you don't have one, something as simple as taking a short walk or dancing alone to a favorite song is enough to help.

70 - Do a repetitive chore. Hand washing dishes, folding clothes, wiping surfaces, etc...

71 - Repetitive hand stitching or weaving. If you're the crafty type.

72 - Head-to-hand writing. Write a page of whatever thoughts that come to mind without stopping.

---

7. https://www.markdownguide.org/

8. https://calmlywriter.com/

9. https://draftin.com/

10. https://gingkoapp.com/

73 - Close your eyes and do nothing for five minutes. This is actually my favorite.

74 - Fight writer's block with free-writing. When facing writer's block, write about it!It may help to start with phrases like, "Right now things aren't going well with my writing project. The problem is __. What drives me crazy is ___. What I want is ___. What I think about this is __."

Once you get started, keep writing whatever comes to mind.

75 - Free-write, even when you're feeling uncertain. When I have no clue what's wrong with a project, I often end up writing something like, "I'm not sure what's wrong with this story, but this about it bothers me..." Often that alone is enough for me to start seeing some answers.

76 - Don't rush to solve your writer's block. After free-writing, I find it works best to stop writing and do something unrelated to writing. What are you usually doing when you're hit with a new idea? Are you taking a walk or showering? Do that instead of writing.

77 - It may take many rounds to fight your writer's block. With this method, I usually have some kind of insight within a day or two. But sometimes, it takes many sessions of free-writing and complaining in my journal to iron out a knotty writing problem. Still, each session illuminates new solutions.

78 - Don't fear change. As you find solutions to your writer's block, you may discover that you will need to make major changes to your writing project—something as big as changing the setting or main characters. Don't fear making those kinds of changes. Although making them is hard, afterward you will feel more aligned with your work. That feeling is worth the discomfort to get there.

79 - Don't give up if your story keeps changing. Since INFPs think non-linearly, we are more prone to experience stories that morph and evolve. The first INFP writer that comes to mind is J.R.R. Tolkien. Publishers pieced his stories together across many editions due to the evolution of his work. The best thing we can do with these kinds of stories is to hold on tight and roll with the punches.

80 - Approach evolving stories with focus. Don't give up if your story keeps changing as you write it. Stick with it, and concentrate on what in that story is valuable to you and what isn't. By thinking about what you enjoy in that story, you can hone in on what should be there, even if it keeps changing. Doing this also makes it easier to know what you need to edit or remove.

81 - Know when to hold on to a story and when to let it go. How do I know that an evolving story isn't one of those stories where I should throw in the towel? Because I'm still interested in it. Lack of interest marks unfinished stories. With evolving stories, there is no lack of interest. It's the vision that keeps changing.

82 - Don't fear being unpredictable. With an evolving story, leaving a trail of broken stories is almost inevitable. This can be a bit scary, especially if you have an online following. It can seem as if you have no clue what you're doing. You start a story, stop, and then change direction with it. If you're posting online, be as transparent and honest as you can about the current situation of your creative process. Your personal struggle with your story is something that other writers can learn from.

And from personal experience, if you're working on a series where the story is changing in this way, don't publish a single book until the story reaches a point of stability.

83 - Skip the boring parts. If you feel bored while writing your draft, your readers will feel bored reading it. If you're starting to write a section that makes you moan within yourself, "Ugh-this is going to be SO BORING..." you may be better off writing a summary of that part and then moving on to the interesting stuff. Put the most effort into what's interesting. Write a short version of the rest.

84 - When feeling bored, realign your work with what's interesting to you. Ask yourself, "Is the next thing I plan to write boring? Is it possible for me to skip or shorten the boring stuff and get to the next exciting thing?" Pay attention to the parts of your writing that are interesting to you. Reduce and remove as much boring as you can.

If the boring part is information that readers need, write it as clearly and succinctly as you can. If you start to lose interest in a project, chances are it has gone off track somewhere and no longer aligns with what motivates you.

85 - Give yourself permission to take a new direction. If you find yourself slogging through a boring story or writing project, stop. Stop writing and re-read what you've written so far. Make note of the last interesting thing you wrote. Experiment with going back and writing again from that point, either skipping the boring stuff or taking your writing in a more interesting direction.

86 - Think about what you enjoy writing and how you enjoy doing it. Take five minutes to meditate on it.

87 - Be patient. Give your natural writing process time to come together.

88 - Mindfully use books and resources on writing. Learning about the processes of other writers can be helpful when you're stuck on your writing project. Yet, be careful not to let the methods of other writers replace the process that naturally works for you.

89 - Test juggling projects. Boredom can come from working on one project at a time. If you feel this way, it's okay to take on another. In fact, I've seen many benefits from having at least two projects going at the same time. This surprised me because for the longest time I've been a "one project at a time only!" person. I still think it's best to focus on one project when it's in the editing stage. I've found that multiple projects work best when I have one large project, like a book or a novel, plus a smaller project like a short story. For more small project ideas, see #33.

90 - Strive to end your story. Despite all the hills and curves you encounter on your writing road trip, keep your main destination in mind—your goal to finish the story. Let the flow of the story dictate the natural ending if possible. And if you find yourself running out of steam, think of the best possible ending you could put on it at the moment.

Some of these tools will work for you. Others won't. The key is to create a set of writing tools that are yours and that helps you get the job done. There is no one "right process" for writing or telling a story. There is simply what works for you and what doesn't. Don't be afraid to learn as you go.

Authentic Sharing

There are times when after ending a writing project, we're glad it's over. We slide our finished work into a drawer intending to never bring it out again to see the light of day. Other times, we finish a writing project, and we know we have to share it. In fact, we won't feel any kind of satisfaction in creating it until we share it with an audience.

In this modern existence, there are so many ways to share a writing project, it can be overwhelming. I think because there are so many options, the biggest pitfall is making things too complicated.

However, you can successfully share your writing in a way that keeps you focused on the next project, instead of being sucked into the social media race and feeling pressure to become an "influencer." You can share your work, and maybe even make a little income.

This chapter is a bit different from the others because it doesn't focus as much on personality type. However, sharing is an important part of the writing process, and I felt if I left this out, this book would be incomplete.

The key to sharing is to keep it simple. When your process is simple, it's easy to repeat. Here are some tips on sending what you write out into the world.

91 - Share finished work with friends. It's possible to get so caught up in sharing our writing with the world, we forget about those we come across every day who could benefit from our work. If you have a family member, friend, or well-regarded acquaintance who you feel would enjoy something you created, share it with them. The easiest way to start building an audience is to start close.

92 - Hold back on sharing your work until you feel you have a grip on it. Having a grip on your work means you are confident with where it is going and at least 80% happy with it. If there are things you don't like, hold off sharing until you make some peace with it.

It's not always possible to have a perfect vision of where your writing is going. It's possible to share something and afterward have to tell those we shared it with, "Uh, sorry. I know my story started out this way, but then I noticed this about it and had to change it."

Although it can be awkward, it's okay to do that. You need to make your writing what you want it to be. Plus, it will help those who read your work to see that writing well involves working with imperfections.

93 - Visit the websites of your favorite authors. This tip is inspired by an exercise from *The Right-Brain Business Plan* by Jennifer Lee.

Write a list of people who create work similar to yours. Then visit their websites and social media. How is their site designed? What do they post? How often do they post? Make notes of your observations. When I did this, I was shocked/thrilled to discover that when it comes to building an author's platform, it's possible to get by with less than you think.

94 - At the bare minimum, have a website with your own domain. Every writer who wants to profit from their work should at least have a website. Your website is the place where readers can go to learn a little bit about you and find your latest books.

There are many tutorials online about how to build a website, so I'm not covering that information. But once you have your site running, at least have the following sections: About Me, My Books, Contact. If you're strapped for money, I recommend looking up services that offer one-page websites. Carrd.co[1] is my favorite one-page site builder, and the pro version is affordable.

95 - On the About Me page, share what kind of writer you are. Tell readers what you write, why you write what you do, and what you hope your writing could do for them. Adding a little tidbit about other things you enjoy outside of writing and your personal sources of inspiration is a nice touch as well.

96 - On the My Books page, share links to your work. This page doesn't have to be titled "My Books." It can be titled "My Work," "My Articles," "My Poetry" or whatever suits what you're making.

97 - On the contact page, give readers a way to connect with you. This can be by social media or the standard contact form that sends messages to your email. I've had the best experiences interacting with readers through email, so I would recommend email over social media.

98 - If you are a writer who makes appearances or runs in-person workshops, also have an events page. Make it easy for your readers to know if you're showing up at their local book store or at a writer's or comic convention.

99 - Blogging is optional. Most of the writers I researched didn't have a blog. Writers who create a wide variety of work blogged little or not at all. Many fiction writers don't blog. So if you're a fiction writer, focus on having a website with the information mentioned previously and an aesthetic that reflects the genres you create in.

100 - Only blog if you love it. Some authors blog a lot, especially if they write non-fiction. If you enjoy writing non-fiction or teaching others, blogging could be for you. Don't blog because others say, "You should have a blog." Only blog if you love creating blog posts. If not, your posts

---

1. https://carrd.co/

won't be that great, and you won't be motivated to improve. As a result, it can end up becoming an energy drain.

Extra Tip: If you set up a one-page website, but decide you want to blog as well, you can actually blog using an email list. Doing the traditional post to a website isn't necessary. In fact, the web service Substack[2] is created for writers who primarily blog through email.

TinyLetter[3] is also good for blogging through email, but Substack stands out because there are no audience limits, and you can set up a membership option. This makes it possible for you to make an income from your posts.

If you want visitors to your site to have access to your past email posts, you can share a link to your public list of past emails in the "My Books/ Work" section of your one-page website. Both TinyLetter and Substack make it easy to share a list of past posts with readers.

Another nice thing about this set up is that you've created a blog and email newsletter in one go.

101 - If you're a writer who creates a wide variety of things, go for a minimalist aesthetic. Some writers have work that is so concentrated on their genre that they can make that the theme of their site. However, I'm not that focused. I've discovered that making my site art gallery inspired, mostly neutrals with pops of color, has made it easier for me to showcase my creative variety. As a writer who creates different things, I've found the site of Lang Leav[4] to be inspiring.

102 - Let go of energy and time drains. There was a time when I would try to regularly post to Twitter and Instagram. Although I enjoyed the interactions, posting was a pain. Scheduling my posts didn't change how

2. https://substack.com/

3. http://tinyletter.com/

4. https://www.langleav.com/books

I felt. Both platforms made me tired. On the other hand, I also share my work to Pinterest and occasionally Bloglovin. When using these sites, I often feel an energy boost. I'm excited to post.

It was a hard decision to make, but I decided to reduce posting to Twitter, and I deleted my Instagram account. I'm not losing traffic to my blog by letting these services go. Twitter and IG brought me the least traffic. It's tough because everyone touts Twitter and Instagram as the ways of being seen, and I fear becoming unseen.

However, the numbers tell a different story. For me, they're not needed.

If you find yourself having to drop some social media accounts because they no longer serve you, but you're not ready to press the delete button, I suggest posting this GIF from Flow Magazine to your account[5], or at least sharing a similar message to your followers.

Fearlessly let go of unnecessary energy drains.

103 - If you decide to blog, you don't have to do it daily. Of the authors I researched, the majority of those who blogged posted once a month, especially if they were focused on creating fiction. Only one author updated his blog daily–Austin Kleon. However, he is a non-fiction writer with a focused collection of published books. Personally, I am a fiction/non-fiction writer with an unfocused collection of published work. That says quite a bit about how I should set up my platform.

104 - What kind of writer are you? Are you focused on a genre or not? That could affect the design of your website. Do you write fiction or non-fiction? That could affect how much you need/want to blog. If you write fiction, it's normal to blog less often than a non-fiction writer, if you decide to blog at all.

---

5. https://www.flowmagazine.com/flow-magazine/made-by-flow/
flow-launches-first-social-media-office.html

105 - Don't let writing new blog posts get in the way of your projects. For a while, I struggled with my internal drive to blog. I'm thinking up new blog posts every day, and when I read a blog post by one of my favorite bloggers, I think, "I want to write an article like that." This would drive me crazy because I felt I was losing my focus.

However, while cleaning my studio, I came across an old journal entry. I was answering journal prompts from the book *INFJ Writer* by Lauren Sapala. The question was, "If you could do a job other than writing stories, what would it be?" My answers were life-style blogger and painter.

Although I know that blogging can pose a risk to my main focus of publishing books, at the same time I know that I need to honor that drive. So now I focus on writing my books during the week and blogging on the weekends. This allows me to scratch that blogging itch without losing focus on my main goal as a writer.

106 - Be aware of your goals. If your primary plan to make an income as a writer involves publishing books and articles for those who are willing to pay you, that needs to be your focus. If your focus is publishing to Wattpad and being supported by BuyMeACoffee, then do that. Focus on your next writing project, not social media.

But if you're a writer who is hoping to mainly make money by teaching online courses, consulting, and coaching others while putting your own writing projects in the backseat, the more traditional blogging as a business approach could work for you.

That means you focus on writing and delivering thoughtful blog posts on at least a weekly basis with eye-catching SEO friendly headlines. Also, these types of bloggers tend to be good at coming up with workbooks, worksheets, and other printables that improve productivity.

However, nothing shows your expertise like having published work, either in book form or through online publications. Personally, I would be willing to take a course from a writer with a nice collection of published works and no blog, because it's still obvious that they are experienced. And if I happen to enjoy their work, then that will make my choice even easier.

107 - Imitate posts you like. When checking out the social media and websites of authors you admire, did you notice what kinds of things they post? What did you like? What didn't you like? Write a list of your observations, good and bad. Then decide what you want and don't want for your social media and blog.

108 - Pay attention to which of your posts are the most popular. If you decided to blog, after about a year you will start to see which posts have the most reads. It's important to pay attention to those posts because those are the ideas that are resonating the most with your visitors. Try to figure out how you can add more to those ideas, maybe updating the old post or even writing new related posts. Doing this will allow you to expand on a topic that is interesting to both you and your audience.

109 - Find the sweet spot. There are three categories of creating stuff. There are things you create that are interesting to you but don't help anyone else. There are things you create purely for others, but don't care about at all. And then there are things you create because they are interesting to you, and those things happen to be helpful to others too.

This is the sweet spot, especially if you plan to sell your work. When you create things that are exciting to you, you have more motivation. When you create things that are also helpful to others, you are pairing that motivation with a larger purpose.

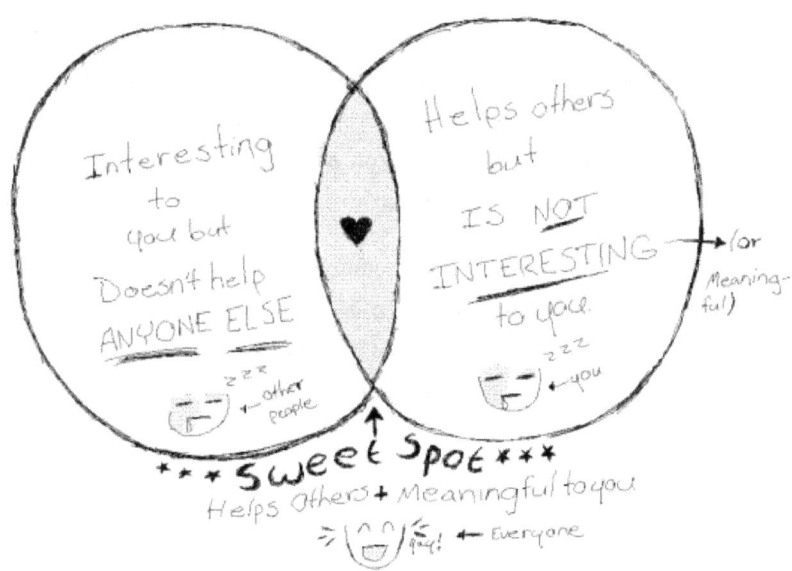

110 - Approach email newsletters with caution. I have struggled with email newsletters so much. I've gone from having a list, to declaring that I will never have a list again, and then back to having a list.

I've given some serious thought as to how I engage with email newsletters. There are only a few that I subscribe to, and I hate websites that hit me with, "Subscribe to MY LIST!" as soon as I visit them. I click the X on those things as soon as possible, and yes, it is annoying. Even if it pops up after a few minutes of reading, it's still irritating.

With that in mind, I decided to treat readers the way I want to be treated, which is, no unnecessary pop-ups on my site. I don't care if marketing gurus say that it converts. I'm not going to assault readers with stuff that I don't like either. This not only goes for how I collect email sign-ups but also for the content of the emails I send.

In the same way as blogging, email newsletters can take precious time away from productive writing. If you are a writer who is focused on publishing, and you want to have a newsletter, it's best to have a newsletter that alerts readers when you have published new work, be it to your blog or a new book, and leave it at that.

Don't give in to being a fancy salesperson if that's not who you are. You don't have to tell your life story with each email. You don't need some elaborate onboarding sequence of emails or offer any kind of free email course (unless you are planning to focus on teaching or coaching others).

All you need to do is let readers know that something new is available and where to read it.

111 - The most important email list is... I've found that the most important email list I have is the one that keeps me in contact with those who have bought my books. Readers to my blog come and go, but those who believed in me enough to invest in my work are truly special.

Not that I don't believe in my regular blog readers, but to me those who buy my work have gone above and beyond.

If you have a blog and are publishing books, don't worry too much about capturing emails of visitors to your site. Instead, put a link at the end of all your published/paid work where readers can subscribe to know when your newest work is available for purchase.

112 - Pay attention to what your audience is doing. So let's say you have an email list at the end of your books, but no one seems to be signing up for it. Then what? You may have to change your approach. Maybe having an email list at the end of your book doesn't fit the mindset of your audience. Maybe things will work better if they can simply sign up to be notified of new work from your blog or social media profile. Avoid being so set on your ideas that you overlook how readers are actually engaging with your writing.

113 - Don't get hung up on email list freebies. The short answer is, you don't need them. If your focus is on staying in touch with those who buy your books and sending them alerts, having an email freebie system isn't necessary. Let the power of your work persuade people to want to hear from you.

When I published *Idealist Dreams,* my focus was to get the book out there. I shared parts of the book to my blog, and that created enough awareness for the book to sell. Super simple and no email freebie necessary.

But one benefit of offering a freebie is that it's a way to stay in touch with those who have not invested in your work but are interested. So it's up to you if you think it's worth communicating with that part of your audience. Also if gathering pre-orders for your book is important to you, having an email freebie can help with that.

Of the 13 writers I researched, only three offered freebies. One internationally famous writer offered a short story and another offered a set of story related printables. One indie writer offered a novella. Offering a PDF sample of a few chapters of your book could also be a good option, especially if you have a link to where readers can pre-order your book at the end of it.

114 - Focus on what you can control. You can't control the number of likes you get. You can control how much you write. You can control how much and how often you publish.

115 - Share your work with online communities where you're already active. I've found the most success when I share my work on social networking sites that I enjoy. I use Pinterest daily, so I decided to use it to promote my work, and it has been great for me. Only do the type of social media that feels light and motivating to you.

If you don't enjoy Facebook or Twitter, don't use it. If you use a social media platform because everyone else is using it, but you're hating the process the entire time, you are not going to communicate well with others on that platform.

116 - It's OK to use one social networking site. I have an ugly confession to make. I used Google Plus. And it was the number one source of traffic for my blog. Well, everyone knows what happened to Google Plus, so I was suddenly bereft of my main way of finding readers. I was worried about how I would recover. However, I knew that I enjoyed using Pinterest, so I decided to lean into that instead.

Pinterest is now the number one source of traffic for my blog, although I also had Twitter, Facebook, and Instagram accounts. I tried updating all of these in tandem, but still, Pinterest came out on top. Over 60% of my readers come from Pinterest and less than 1% from the other three. The rest of my readers find me through Google Search.

Clearly, anything other than Pinterest is a waste of time for me. So I deleted Facebook and Instagram but held on to Twitter. For now...

The lesson I've learned? I've learned that it's OK to lean on one social media site. If the one you rely on goes down, it's fairly easy to recover. It does take some patience and willingness to learn to move to a new platform, but the recovery isn't as painful as we imagine. Losing your followers is not the end of the world.

I also feel that social media works better if you give the majority of your energy to one service. Then you can focus on giving your followers a better experience on that specific platform. That's harder to do when you're split across multiple accounts. You are trying to do it all, but end up doing none of it well.

117 - Share what you appreciate and love. For a long time, I struggled with what to share on social media. I would look up 30-day post challenges and calendars on Pinterest. However, little did I know that Pinterest actually held the secret to making good social media posts. And it wasn't in those pre-planned post calendars.

If you don't know what to post, simply share what you love or appreciate that day. If you come across a quote you love or an article that touched your heart, share it. If you have a favorite coffee cup, ink pen, or notebook, share those.

Did you write a fantastic sentence? Share it. If you love your newest published work or feel nostalgic about an older piece, share that. Share stuff from friends who are close to you, and from bloggers and social media accounts that you appreciate. Share books, movies, and music that you enjoy. Share sights in nature that touch you.

Share all that's beautiful to you.

118 - Try scheduling your posts. When I was attempting to post to Instagram regularly, I found scheduling posts helpful. Using a scheduling service gave me time to fine-tune my descriptions and tags.

When I was using Blogger, I would schedule my blog posts, and I appreciated the extra time that gave me to make adjustments to my work before it went live. As introverts, we need those extra moments to adjust our words and make sure everything is almost perfect.

I enjoyed using Planoly for Instagram. I've heard many others say that they enjoy using Later. Although I use Pinterest, I do not schedule my pins. I simply create a new one every time I have a new blog post.

I don't have a ton of followers. Still for some reason, my pins have a wide-reaching impact, so this has been working well enough for me.

119 - Think about how your writing helps others. Knowing how you are helpful can make it easier to share what you do with others, online or in person. Not only will it give you a clear way of describing what you do, but it can also give you guidance on how to approach future writing projects. Writing projects that make an impact hit that sweet spot of being enjoyable to you and helpful to others.

So go ahead and write a list. Title it, "How I am helpful to others." Write about how your writing helps others. What does it help them do? What does it help them learn? What does it help them feel?

120 - Fiction writers, think about how your writing is helpful. Don't mentally check out on this paragraph, fiction writers! I've seen the idea of being helpful applied mainly to non-fiction writers. But recently, I've discovered that my fiction writing also helps others. Fiction writers help by creating what readers wish to feel.

If you're writing fiction, how do you want your readers to feel? What do you want to see in stories? How does your writing help others who want to see the same thing? When working with fiction, the vision of how you are helpful can get muddy, so it's helpful to write it out and refer to it regularly.

As a short example, with my fiction I try to help others feel positive and empowered. My writing also helps audiences who want to see multicultural characters and meaningful friendships.

So yes, your fiction can most definitely help others! But it takes a little bit of extra awareness to see how.

121 - Deep audience analysis is not necessary. When figuring out the audience for our writing, it's common to hear advice such as figuring out how old they are, where they live, how much money they make...In reality though, you can do without those details. Instead ask yourself, "Who can I help with what I currently write?" When you focus on who you can help, details such as age, location, and so on tend to come together on their own.

122 - Focus on the current you, not the future you. Notice that the keyword is "current." As an INFP, I often get caught in a time warp. At times, I've focused too much on how I can help others based on my future goals. As a result, I fail to see how my future goals affects my helpfulness.

For example, let's say I want to learn CSS for website design. As a beginner, I can't actively help other CSS programmers or create complex things. But in my unrealistic mental world, I think, "It would be cool to be able to share a website template as soon as I can," although that's way beyond my current abilities.

However, if I focused on where I am currently instead of the future, I would end up writing about my learning journey and get support from others. I won't be helpful to experienced programmers, but I would be helpful to other beginners.

Focusing too much on the future can leave you trying to write like a professional on a subject you're starting to learn about.

Along those lines, I also wish to write science fiction or fantasy. But the reality is that right now, all my published work is contemporary, and currently, I'm writing contemporary short fiction and loving it. Maybe one day, I'll become that sci-fi fantasy writer, but that's not who I am right now.

123 - Focus on the current you, not the past you. Just as the future can get you into trouble, obsessing over how you were helpful in the past can hurt too.

About five years ago, I was deeply involved in creating a webcomic. At the time, my blog was about my process of creating comics and other webcomic makers found that helpful.

Now my focus has shifted to writing. I could write about designing characters and pages now, but I would be less helpful because that's not the current role I'm playing.

So when looking at how you help others, stay focused on where you are now at this moment. Not on who you were or who you will be. When you focus on how you are helpful now with what you currently have, you will always be helpful to others.

124 - Write to audiences that you already belong to. I enjoy reading Japanese shoujo manga. I enjoy it so much, that when I had a story idea for a webcomic, I created it with shoujo readers in mind. In it are niche references and common tropes that only regular readers of manga would catch.

That was five years ago, and now my finished webcomic is a thing of the past. However looking back, I realize that if I wasn't a huge fan of shoujo comics, I wouldn't have been able to create something that so many people enjoyed.

According to the article **How to Sell Profitable Digital Products** on Podia.com[6], it is 1,000 times harder to sell to an audience when you are not an insider.

---

6. https://www.podia.com/articles/create-profitable-product

So let's make things easy. Ask yourself, "What audiences/groups am I a part of?" Writing a list helps. You will find that some of your categories will be broad, such as which generation you identify with or where you live. Some will be narrow, such as Yorkie owners or highly sensitive INFPs.

After making that list, think "How can I use my writing to help others in my audience?"

In the end, sharing is truly about caring. When you share what you write, focus on helping those who come into contact with your work. And when readers reach out to you, always respond, always be kind, and always show gratitude. They don't have to read and enjoy your stuff, but they do.

The days of being the writer locked away in an ivory tower and publishing work to the faceless masses are over. Today, writing is personal.

Dealing with Feedback & Improving

When you share your work, getting feedback is unavoidable. That is part of the risk of putting yourself out there. But taking the chance to share something valuable with others even in the face of naysayers is worth it! Don't let the fear of feedback cripple you from sharing things that others need. Readers need your writing.

Feedback also opens you up to growth and improvement. Let that feedback, positive or negative, spur you to get better.

Here are some more specific tips on dealing with feedback and improving your craft.

125 - Give yourself time to digest criticism. When I was publishing my webcomic, I faced a ton of feedback. Much of it fell into two categories: reactions to the plot and criticism of my art. The hardest to handle was criticism of my art. I had art skills, but I had never created that much comic art before, and creating comics requires a unique skill set. And there were other issues that were causing my art not to come out so great, such as learning how to create art digitally.

But instead of firing back at criticism, I stepped away from the computer and did something else. Yeah, I felt frustrated at the comments, but distancing myself gave me time to think about what the words said. As my emotions cooled down, I could see the value in the criticism. I had room for improvement, and I took the suggestions.

When facing criticism, give yourself time to find some calm. Then think, "How can I improve?"

126 - Embrace helpful criticism. One thing about the webcomic community is that much of the criticism is helpful. My art improved, and I was able to tell an exciting story thanks to the wonderful feedback from readers. The best kind of criticism helped me to improve the fundamentals of my craft—my drawings and story presentation.

The least helpful feedback was suggestions of what to do next in my story. If you are publishing serialized work online, take reader suggestions on the plot with a grain of salt. First, this is your story, not theirs! Creating the plot is what you do. If they want a story with a different direction, they need to go write their own. Second, following reader suggestions can make your story less interesting. You don't want that.

Yet, the best thing about reader feedback is that it gives you a window into the thoughts of your audience. My favorite comments on my comic were things like, "Oh, I know where this is going!" and then the reader would detail what they thought was going to happen next. If they were wrong, I was super excited. If they were right, I would go with what I had planned, but tweak it so they would only be half-right.

When it comes to nonfiction, reader feedback helps me see what I need to write next. As a result, not only do I create books that I enjoy writing, but I also hit the sweet spot of what others need.

Don't fear feedback. The majority of it is insightful. And this is coming from a sensitive introvert who has a history of anxiety and depression. It's not that bad.

127 - Keep in mind your personal vision for your work. No creative project is 100% complete. You can always add more and change things. Feedback from your audience highlights that. But while improving your work, don't forget what is you. Since we can always add to what we create, we risk manipulating things so much that it no longer reflects our original vision.

So regardless of the feedback you get, keep in mind the purpose of your writing project. Then only follow the advice that supports the grand vision for your work—not water it down.

128 - Copy your favorites. After finishing my last webcomic, I found myself facing the worst artist's block ever. I continued to create art, but none of it felt right. Drawing was no longer relaxing, and I felt my confidence sinking, even after creating art that was technically sound. Something important was missing.

One day I watched a video class on Creative Live hosted by Kate Bingaman-Burt entitled *Drawing the Everyday Every Day*. That class introduced me to a simple art exercise where you pick a few items from your bag and draw them.

For the first time in a long time, I had a lot of fun drawing. Next thing I knew, I was drawing objects I found in my desk drawers. I was addicted!

I reclaimed my inner fire for visual art by copying elements of what I love and arranging them into something new.

Imitation got me out of my rut. If you find yourself in a writing rut, copying and paying attention to what inspires you can help.

Copy your favorite

- Sentences, paying attention to structure

- Words

- Descriptions

Try rearranging them. What kind of writing can you make from these words?

Experiment with copying, yet twisting things to sound more you. How would YOU describe that kind of setting? That kind of character?

129 - Keep a growth mindset. Never think you know it all. There is always more to learn about the craft of writing from the basics to the business side of things.

And even if you don't care about selling your writing, continuing to learn will keep you interested in what you create. When you have the mindset that there is always something more to learn, writing will always be fresh.

130 - Change one thing about your process. After using the same process for drawing over 500 comic pages, I felt unchallenged. Using the same old process made it hard for me to bring new things to my work, and I knew I had to do something different.

But in trying to reinvent myself, I went too far. I changed the software I used and my style. Instead of reinvigorating me, I felt overwhelmed, and this made my artist block even worse.

Looking back I see that in wanting to change my process, I was on the right track. But, instead of changing everything, I should have changed only one thing.

If you are getting tired of your writing, is there one thing you can change about your process? Could you try writing by hand instead of typing? Could you experiment with creating a short piece of work that is different from what's normal for you?

131 - Combine your writing with other mediums. Doing so helps you to stretch your writing skills and grow. Play with combining your writing with music, art, or video.

Dabble in the medium that you would like to combine your writing with. Even if you are no good at drawing or making music, trying it out will at least help you to better understand the writing needs of that medium.

132 - Try different forms of writing. If you write fiction, give nonfiction a try. If you write nonfiction, try creating a short story or poetry. Exploring will give you something fresh to bring to each work you create. Also if you plan on being an indie or freelance writer, having a variety of skills will make it easier to earn an income.

133 - Learn something simple that's unrelated to writing. Never knitted before? Learn the basics and create the simplest project you can. Experimenting with new disciplines will give you fresh perspectives. As a result, you will enrich your writing and find unexpected inspiration.

134 - Learn about different plot structures. Let go of sticking to one kind of plot framework for your stories. By testing a variety of simple plot structures, you will end up creating your own personal set of plotting tools. Then you will have what you need to build stories without them being cookie-cutter.

135 - Take a moment to bring together all your stories, finished and unfinished. Read and enjoy them. Appreciate the value of what you've already created and the lessons learned. With each thing you make, you are building your life's body of work.

136 - Don't rush to throw out old or unfinished work. Instead, try combining works together to see if you can create something new.

137 - Know when to throw out old work. After reading *Goodbye Things* by Fumio Susaki, I appreciated how letting go of my old stuff can release my creativity. I'm not talking about a thoughtless, "Throw out all the undone projects!" Instead, I realized that:

• Some unfinished projects no longer reflect who I am.

• Some unfinished projects no longer reflect what I want.

• I can make unfinished projects into something new, but remixing isn't appealing when there's an overwhelming amount of them.

It's also hard to create something new from a project you don't care about.

So, let go of old work that doesn't excite you or that no longer represents who you are. If there are parts of it you like, save whatever good parts you can, and let it go.

138 - Give yourself time. Nothing grows overnight. Introverts need more time alone to process things. Introverted Feeling needs time and space to sort things out. It may even feel like you're wandering. Don't let that scare you. You are not as lost as you feel. Don't rush yourself.

Introverted Feeling needs time to determine how your writing projects fit with your core values.

139 - Give yourself a life-time. INFPs tend to build large collections of creative work over their lifetime. At 16 personalities.com[1], famous INFPs include J.R.R. Tolkien, William Shakespeare, Bjork, Alicia Keys, and Julia Roberts. I also want to add Audrey Hepburn to that list. And guess what? All these people have crafted huge bodies of work that span decades. I find this super exciting and motivating. I'm still young, and I'm only getting started.

Yet regardless of your age, it's never too late to build that personal body of creative work that is unique to you.

---

1. https://www.16personalities.com/infp-personality

Using Functions in Your Writing Practice: Quick Reference

Let's take a short imaginary journey through your mind...

Introverted Feeling (Fi)

I digest the emotions that well up within you. The circumstances that evoked these emotions are placed into my internal values system. Is this good or bad?

Making Use of Introverted Feeling (Fi)

> · Express feelings and deeply held values. Write them down. Make them into art.

> · Take time to vividly imagine yourself in the shoes of someone else. See if you can imagine the viewpoints of two different people at once.

> · Write about something you are passionate about.

> · Think about if your writing feels good to you or not.

> · Take time to enjoy the happiness that comes from creating writing that expresses your values.

> · Editing with Introverted Feeling: Does the mood feels right? Does it create the emotions I want to feel? Is this a true representation of my values?

Extroverted Intuition (Ne)

I connect ideas and create representations of emotions and values. Sadness is like coming to the end of an ice cream cone. No sadness is more like a rainy day. Or it's like when you're stabbed in the back by a friend. This could be shown in a painting. A story. A poem. A song? Maybe all of the above...

Once Introverted Feeling decides what is valuable, Extroverted Intuition gets to work creating possible ways these feelings and ideas can be expressed.

Making Use of Extroverted Intuition

· Stay aware of relationships and connections.

· Look for external experiences that create an emotional impact, such as music, movies, or anything else you enjoy.

· Talking out ideas can help.

· Be aware that parts of your project may arrive in pieces, not as a whole. Be prepared to write anywhere.

· Use Extroverted Intuition to collect information on the craft of writing and look for the connections between different methods.

· Extroverted Intuition is great to have while writing, but a pain in the butt while editing. It keeps adding new ideas, which isn't the point of the editing process.

Introverted Sensing (Si)

These ideas remind me of the sadness and isolation you felt when you moved away from your childhood home.

Extroverted Intuition (butts in): Yes, and this NEW short story can be about someone on a rainy day who bought some ice cream before finding out their friend stabbed them in the back, creating feelings of loss like when I left my childhood home, and then..."

Making Use of Introverted Sensing

- Introverted Sensing combines past experiences and feelings with the more recent discoveries of Extroverted Intuition.

- Introverted Sensing arranges events into something that makes sense based on past experience. Good for filling plot holes.

- Introverted Sensing lends itself to order and consistency. Use it to create writing routines and rituals.

- Introverted Sensing is happy looking back at what has been accomplished. Print and save stories. Create a personal library to see visually what has been made.

- Take breaks by using Introverted Sensing. Work on crafts. Do some solo exercise.

- Editing with Introverted Sensing: Does this fit established patterns of writing? Are there any plot holes or missing information that the reader needs?

Extroverted Thinking (Te)

I'm ready to get things done! I'll make plans with Si to work on this every day!

Si: Writes every day. Demands to have some kind of self-care (walking, exercise, tea, coffee, nap) in exchange.

Te: We're making progress! We're headed towards the goal! I am so the boss.

Fi: Great! This fits with what I feel and value.

Ne: Could we stop for a moment? I have more ideas! (Te presses hands over ears and hums...)

Making Use of Extroverted Thinking

· Set simple goals and flexible deadlines. If the goal isn't reached, readjust.

· Try framing goals as challenges. Nanowrimo is a good example.

· Use Extroverted Thinking to critique your work and cut out what isn't needed.

· Editing with Te: Does this make logical sense in the context of my story? Is this information necessary? Can I streamline my writing more? Is it easy to understand? How are the writing mechanics? Critique.

Recommended Resources & Conclusion

For a long time, I refused to read books about the craft of writing. I thought, "Why should I read about writing when I could be writing?" I believed that reading fiction and comics was the best way to learn how to write.

But the year I published my webcomic, self-publishing was growing fast. I knew I had to learn more about this new opportunity. I read books about self-publishing fiction. That transitioned to reading more about writing fiction. I find most books on writing not to be as helpful as I wish. Still, there is a handful of books that made a lasting impact on me.

That's not the fault of the authors of these books. The thing is that not all books on writing fit who I am as a writer. When reading about writing, it's important to find books that add more to who you already are. It's been a difficult search, but I've found books that have made an impact because they fit the way I handle information as an INFP.

So here are my favorite books and helpful resources on writing with some commentary. The first few resources are especially helpful if you want to start making money as an indie writer. The rest are for improving your craft. I hope this list will help you begin your journey of finding writing resources that fit you.

Paused to Prolific by K Webster

After writing *How I Learned to Plan as an INFP*, I realized that I felt ready to try to make writing at least a part-time job.

But my writing habits were the same as when I was in high school. As I worked on this book and a few other projects, I could not stop agonizing over how unfocused and slow I was. I don't mean slow in the way of being thoughtful as I worked on my projects. I mean slow as in feeling like I was slogging through a mud pit.

Paused to Prolific helped me to get out of the pit and start making the kind of progress that feels good to me. This book also forced me to grow up as a writer. For the longest time, I resisted word-tracking.

But this book helped me to see that word-tracking is what professional writers do. Word-tracking helps writers to see their progress and better understand their process.

Being accountable for my word count was one of the most difficult things I've had to do so far as a writer. I don't know why, but noting down my word count for the day was painful, although it's such a simple thing to do. The pain was from learning how to be more responsible for my output. Going through this book has set me up to be a better writer for life.

Also, Webster's techniques fit well with the way INFPs tend to think. Her method of juggling four different drafts at the same time fits with my natural habit of starting more than I can finish. At first working on so many drafts seemed crazy, but I was amazed at how quickly I adapted to it.

She shares how she created a "mix-tape" book of her unfinished, B-side worthy stories, good inspiration for writers who struggle with finishing projects. Plus I appreciate her suggestion to use unfocused moments to think more about writing projects. Browsing Pinterest to build up your book does have a place in the writing process.

Read *Paused to Prolific* if you want to get your distractions under control, write regularly, and get writing done in a way that is fun and empowering. Plus it's a quick read and will get you back on track in no time.

Grammarly[1]

After editing a piece of writing as well as you can, run it through Grammarly. Since January of 2020, I've been running all of my blog posts through Grammarly, and I wish I would have done it sooner.

Simbi[2]

As a writer, especially when you're first starting out, there may be some services you can't afford. I love designing covers for my books, but for other writers, this isn't their thing. Along with the visual design, bringing a book to life also involves editing and proofreading.

Simbi is wonderful because it allows you to trade services with other people, bypassing the need to have a lot of money in the bank to publish a book. Working with others in this way has helped me to grow so much as a writer. I was able to work with a wonderful business coach that helped me get back on track with publishing my work—a service that I do not have enough money for at this moment.

Simbi also helped me to launch my 20 Minute 1-on-1 Writing Workshop, which I'm no longer offering, but it was cool to see that I could help others improve their writing as well.

Use Simbi if you need help, but don't have the money.

Draft2Digital[3]

Draft2Digital is the easiest way to publish your work. With little stress, you can take what you write from a basic Word Document to a published ebook. Also, they have features that work in the favor of indie writers. I am a huge fan of their Universal Book Links. This feature makes it easy

---

1. https://app.grammarly.com/

2. https://simbi.com/

3. https://www.draft2digital.com/

for me to share all the links to my books no matter how many retailers are selling it.

Read their formatting handbook before getting started. It's straightforward and chances are you can set up a Word Document that's D2D ready to type your draft in. Then you won't have to worry about formatting it later.

Use Draft2Digital if you want to publish an ebook without the pain.

7 steps to move your work online[4] - a blog post by Louisa Deasey

After writing your book, I recommend following the steps in this blog post. It will walk you through setting up a website, an email list, and letting everyone know about your new book in the simplest way possible. I used this post as a guide in launching this book that you are reading right now.

I am not new to having an online presence, but I appreciated the simple approach in this post. Most of the time, this kind of advice is given in an over-complicated way.

The gem in this post is the encouragement to share free samples of your finished work. Deasey suggests sharing your samples in exchange for email sign-ups. If you need to build a following fast, I definitely believe this is the most efficient (and considerate) way to do it.

With Canva or Word (or a combination of both), you can make a nice PDF sample. Make sure to link to your published book at the end of the sample so readers can buy it. Then share that sample as widely as you can: as a blog post, on social media, and to anyone else who you think would be interested.

---

4. https://louisadeasey.com/7-steps-to-move-your-work-online/

Although offering a sample this way is a great idea, especially if you're in a pinch, I've found in my experience that it's not always necessary. For this book and the two before it, I've shared samples without asking for email addresses in return.

I've done this by creating blog posts related to the content of my books, linking them to my published books, and then sharing to Pinterest.

One nice thing about offering samples without requesting an email address is that it lowers the barrier for new readers. They can get to know me and my work before investing in it.

Although it is a simple thing, when you ask people for their email address, you are asking for an investment—you're asking for permission to take a bit of their time and attention. With the high volume of emails people receive, I respect that an email address may be too much for some to give.

Should you share a sample of a book that's not yet published? I stand with K. Webster on this issue. If it's a draft, don't share it. If it's in early edit, don't share it. If all you have left is some proofreading and final formatting, then it's okay to share. Like Webster, I too have been burned by presenting drafts as soon-to-be-finished work so many times, and I don't want you to experience that!

If your sample is from a book that is yet to be published, add a link to where your readers can pre-order your book if they want to buy it.

Read *7 Steps to Move Your Work Online* if you need a quick guide on setting up a website and sharing your work with the world.

The Chic Author by Fiona Farris

There is nothing like unexpectedly discovering a book sibling! By the way, a book sibling is a book written by someone else that is the perfect companion to one of your published books.

If you need more help after reading this book, I highly recommend reading this one next, regardless of your gender.

In many ways her book is similar to this one, but she also brings out some extra insights that you may find helpful.

I like how this book shares tips on

- Making use of an inspiration notebook
- Breaking a draft into workable parts
- Using Microsoft Word or a similar application for writing, if that's your thing
- Embracing your writing style and overcoming fear, especially if publishing is your goal
- Spending no money (or at least less than $20) to publish and market your book

I also appreciate how she openly shares that she self-edits before publishing and has only used an outside editor a few times.

Her openness about this has also given me the boldness to stand up and say, "I self-edit too."

As someone who can't afford to pay a small fortune for editing, reading her experience validated my practice of editing my own books. It's okay to self-edit, but make sure to do it well.

When I was in college, I paid $100+ for a textbook that was riddled with typos. It was so irritating, that I took out my trusty red pen and started writing corrections in the margins and adding punctuation. I think the editor took a vacation...

Having the resources doesn't always result in a high quality book.

I'm looking forward to seeing how this book impacts my writing process and helps me grow.

Read *The Chic Author* by Fiona Farris if you want learn how to write non-fiction with ease, and put your best foot forward when introducing your self-published book to the world.

You Poet by Rayna Hutchison and Samuel Blake

Poet or not, this is one of my favorite books for the modern writer. What I love about this book is how it acknowledges the role of social media in publishing, and how to use that to your advantage.

Plus this book gives a concise overview of the essentials of writing. It starts with exercises to help you find your voice. Then it goes into essential writing tools, such as grammar basics, similes and metaphors, word choice, and editing. Finally, it has writing prompts for practice, advice on getting over writer's block, and tips for publishing online—especially publishing short works using social media.

Read *You Poet* if you need a quick refresher on the writing basics and inspiration for sharing your work to social media like an always fresh Instapoet. It's a great quick reference for the modern writer.

How to Create a Microbusiness That Matters Course by Courtney Carver[5]

If you are an INFP writer with multipotential, you are going to love this course.

It can be difficult to tie together a variety of pursuits. But this course helped me to see that focusing on how I can be helpful right now is the key to bringing my passions together into something that makes sense. I

---

5. https://bemorewithless.com/micro/

love how in her course she says that it's good to have too many ideas. That means you have a lot to give.

As a polymath, I have many skill sets. Yet, not all of them are developed enough to help others. This course helped me to focus on using my most developed and helpful skills to start creating my fledgling business as a writer/artist.

What I also appreciate about this course is how it laser focuses on what matters when it comes to creating a business. It's built around what you want in your work life, the skills you have, and how those skills are helpful to others. Since her course centers around business as an act of giving, it has helped me to grow professionally and personally.

One important thing I want to point out is that in the course, she doesn't recommend using your name for a website address.

However, as a writer, it's best if you do. Using your name in your website's domain name makes it easy for readers to find you, and in the business of writing, that's important. This is especially true if you plan on writing fiction.

But overall, I love this course! Not only is it effective, but it's also simple. It can be completed over a weekend.

Take the *How to Create a Mircobusiness that Matters* course if you want to improve your business as a writer/(insert other occupations here).

A Writer's Space by Eric Maisel

This book is about more than setting up a nice writing desk. Out of all the books on this list, I mention Maisel's book the most in my blog posts. This book not only covers setting up physical writing spaces but also mental spaces. His chapter on writing in bed is fantastic (by the way, I created most of my webcomic in bed. I feel no shame).

His chapter on morphing stories has had a lasting impact on how I deal with stories that keep changing. In this book, I've referred to such stories as "evolving stories." He also introduces a fascinating way of plotting fiction by following characters as they interact with their environment.

This concept ended up being a major influence on how I decided to plot a recent work in progress.

Read *A Writer's Space* if you want to build a writing habit, have a writing environment that suits you, and are dealing with a story that is constantly changing.

Writing With Out Rules by Jeffery Somers

This book is as if *Paused to Prolific* by K. Webster and *A Writer's Space* by Eric Maisel had a baby.

Like K. Webster, Somers also expresses the importance of being able to juggle many drafts at the same time. He also has a nice chapter with tips on how to combine, remix, and revamp unfinished work. Similar to Maisel's book, what he shares about plotting is soothing to the souls of those who fall between pantsing and plotting. In fact, he calls it "Plantsing."

Plantsing involves using the writing method that comes naturally to you first. If you're a plotter, you create your plot and then start writing. If you're a pantser, then you start writing as you normally do.

But when you get stuck, that's when you switch methods. If you are a natural pantser, when you get stuck, stop writing and create a simple outline to get back on track. If you are a plotter, when you get stuck, abandon the outline and write whatever comes to mind.

I tried this with a short story I'm working on, and this method worked for me (I'm a plotter, by the way).

This suggestion helped me to see my fiction writing in a new light, and I'm thankful for that. I also appreciate his suggestions on creating plots in general with a focus on watching how a character navigates their environment, like the method of Eric Maisel.

There is much more I can say about this book, but what stands out to me the most is the encouragement to embrace your personal process. Regardless of what that process is, you can learn to make it work.

Read *Writing Without Rules* if you're ready to let go of ideas of how writers "should work" and lean into what works for you.

INFJ Writer by Lauren Sapala

If you want to know more about how much of an impact being an intuitive introvert has on your writing, read this book. I appreciate how Sapala sheds light on the writing process of INFPs. Her suggestions may or may not help you, but having more awareness can go a long way. Reading this book helped me to have a clearer picture of what kind of writing advice I needed.

Read *INFJ Writer* if you want a nice start to understanding how personality type affects your writing.

Wild Mind: Living the Writer's Life by Natalie Goldberg

Similar to Steven King's book *On Writing*, this book blurs the line between writing advice and memoir. But for the way my mind works, I found Goldberg's advice and insights on the writing life more helpful. After reading her book, I came away from it thinking, "I'll never say I don't know what to write about EVER again."

My favorite takeaways from her book are her " writing rules" and practice prompts. They are so simple, it's liberating. She shows how practice can grow into works of creative writing. Her concept of writing practice helped me to fix the biggest problems in my current WIP.

I also love how she explains the power of reading what you write aloud, either to yourself or to an audience. Plus, her thoughts on writing style reflects how I feel about style—that style is who you are. She describes writing style as "our individual experiences being digested."

Read *Wild Mind* if you want a more flexible and intuitive writing life and inspiration while between writing projects.

Fearless Writing by William Kenower

Writing is more than sitting your butt in a chair and typing stuff. It involves conflicting emotions. What I enjoy about *Fearless Writing* is how it highlights the emotional conflicts of writing and what to do about them.

I also like how this book expresses that writing with emotional impact is in some ways more important than plot. You can have a story with a lot of exciting stuff going on, but if it doesn't make the reader feel something, what's the point?

Read *Fearless Writing* if you want to get a handle on your emotions toward writing and put emotions on display in your writing.

Story Trumps Structure by Steven James

This is the first writing book that made me feel that as a writer, my process is not that strange. I was thrilled to learn that other writers who approach storytelling similar to me do exist.

The way James plots his stories is almost exactly the way I plan most of mine, with a few differences. I do have some criticism for certain parts of the book, but to me his chapters in the section *The Secrets to Organic*

Writing are amazing. I wrote more about his book in my blog post, Using Writer's Intuition to Write Fiction[6].

It was as if I was seeing my process for the first time.

Read *Story Trumps Structure* if you are in that awkward spot of being both a plotter and a pantser.

Brevity: A Flash Fiction Handbook by David Galef

I've already mentioned the joy of doing short writing projects a few times already. If doing short work appeals to you, but you don't know where to start, this is the book to read. My favorite thing about this book is how it gives a broad view of how to write flash fiction. Short works of writing do not mean less impact.

Read *Brevity* if you want to get a jumpstart in creating short fiction.

L'art de la Liste by Dominique Loreau

As writers, we have to manage a ton of information. There's information for writing projects. There's our personal writing practice and journaling. There's our own habit of reading and the notes that creates. Plus we also want to hold on to ideas and observations. It can all become a crazy mess of stuff!

L'Art de la List is a good guide on how to record and bring all that together without becoming overwhelmed. Lists are the secret to saving information that matters in a form that is concise and easy to find.

Although this isn't a writing book, it's one that writers need to read because the list-creating techniques in it can help busy writers to:

· Capture ideas and observations

---

6. https://arcadiapage.com/2018/11/using-writers-intuition-to-write-fiction.html

· Have a simple journaling practice

· Have a simple regular writing practice, from testing out descriptions to imaginary conversations

· Manage research and information

· Plan stories

If you're also an artist, creating lists is an easy way to bring your writing and art together. This book holds a ton of advice on making lists work for you. Plus as an INFP, working with lists helps me to see how different ideas connect. Being aware of patterns is a major part of how we process information.

But my favorite advice from this book involves how to organize lists.

Loreau advises having your list-making practice divided into two parts: capture and organization.

Have one notebook for capturing.

Notebooks are perfect for the capturing process. Go about your life and jot down whatever comes to mind. Title and date the entries in your notebook to keep this information somewhat organized.

Use a computer or binder system for creating long-term/archival lists and organizing them for storage.

At least once a day, make time to look through what you've jotted down. Decide what you want to save and let go. From what you save, create new lists to keep for the long term.

Use the topic as the title and date the lists. I type my lists and save them to my computer. If you're a paper person, it's best to keep to one list per page in-case you want to add more to it later.

Creating archival lists is also a great time to add artwork, photos, and other embellishments, inspired by what you captured.

If you are a Bullet Journaller, this is one of the most exciting ways I've come across so far for archiving. Go through your Bullet Journal and copy the information that you want to keep to lists.

Add those lists to your digital or paper archive, stored in alphabetical order. Then let go of the rest.

This method also removes the pressure of making your notebook pretty. Your notebook is for capturing. Bullet Journaling is for capturing. So yes, it's going to be crazy and ugly. That's the nature of it. But when you go back and create your archival lists, then you can make them as beautiful and perfect as you want.

Loreau recommends using a computer or a binder system for storing lists. It's important to be able to add to the lists without running out of space. Also, it's best if your lists are portable so you can carry any information needed with you. She recommends half-page sized binders or smaller. She didn't mention this in her book, but index cards could also work for this.

One tip on reading this book: don't let her list suggestions overwhelm you.

Lists can grow new lists on their own. The key is to look at each entry in your list as having the potential of becoming a whole new list. With this kind of approach, you will create a collection of lists that fit your needs because they build on other lists you've made.

Read *L'art de la Liste* if you are a writer who is struggling to manage all the information that comes from being a writer.

What These Books Have in Common

The books on this list are about exploring the writing process. They all contain helpful thoughts and exercises, but no ridged "blueprints and plans" for success. The writing method that is natural for you is the best writing method for success.

These books...

Focus on emotion and discovery.

Give support to writers who don't write in order.

Highlight the daily side of writing life.

Gives useful insights on unfinished work.

Contain flexible rules and encourage writing fluidity.

All writing matters and can grow. I can't wait to see what you, dear INFP writer, will create.

Note from the Author

Thank you so much for reading this book and supporting me on my author's journey! My deepest hope is that this book will support you as well. Writing is never done in isolation, even if your best friends are books while you pound away at the keyboard.

If you purchased this book from a retailer with a review system, please leave an honest review. Doing so will make my book more visible for others who could benefit from this information.

And if you purchased this book from my website, why thank you very much! If you think what you've read will be helpful to anyone you know, please share the link with them.

Do you have any thoughts or comments on what you've read and enjoyed? Feel free to contact me at arcadia@arcadiapage.com. I'd love to hear what you've found helpful.

Take care & with much love,

Arcadia Page

Don't miss out!

Visit the website below and you can sign up to receive emails whenever Arcadia Page publishes a new book. There's no charge and no obligation.

https://books2read.com/r/B-A-XZED-NPHJB

BOOKS 2 READ

Connecting independent readers to independent writers.

Also by Arcadia Page

Idealist Dreams: How I Learned to Plan as an INFP
I Want to Do All the Things: Finding Balance as a Polymath,
Multipotentialite & Renaissance Soul
I Can't Help Being an INFP Writer

Watch for more at www.arcadiapage.com.

About the Author

Arcadia Page is a writer and artist from central Florida. When she's not writing, she enjoys drawing, reading, and crafting. She shares her life with her husband, who also enjoys writing stories.

Read more at www.arcadiapage.com.